Penguin Modern European Poets
Advisory Editor: A. Alvarez

Selected Poems · Juan Ramón Jiménez, Antonio Machado

Juan Ramón Jiménez – Nobel Prize winner – was born in Moguer, Andalucía in 1881, and is considered to be a central figure in contemporary Spanish poetry. The successor of Rubén Darío in the development of modernism, his work shows many French influences, and he has been the greatest poetical influence in that brilliant school of modern Spanish poetry of which F. Garcia Lorca was one of the younger members. There is nothing in Jiménez of the conventional Andalusian pose known as *Popularismo*, so important in the poetry of some of his contemporaries, though he is no less fundamentally Spanish. He lived his later years in the U.S.A. and Puerto Rico and died in 1958.

Antonio Machado died in 1939 at the age of sixty-four. As a boy he went to school in Madrid, became involved in its literary life in the 1890s and published some satirical comments on the social and literary scene in 1893. On a visit to Paris in 1899 he met Oscar Wilde and Moréas. A teacher of French by profession, he married his landlady's daughter in 1909, and his personal happiness coupled with a new concern for Spanish problems helped to liberate his poetry from its early *tristesse*. His wife, however, died tragically in 1912 and Machado became increasingly melancholic with an ironic, cryptic note creeping into his poetry. A staunch Republican at the time of the Civil War, he died in exile in France.

Deborah Hale.

Selected Poems

Juan Ramón Jiménez

Translated by
J. B. Trend *and* J. L. Gili
with an Introduction by
J. B. Trend

Antonio Machado

Translated by
Charles Tomlinson
and Henry Gifford
with an Introduction by
Henry Gifford

Penguin Books

Penguin Books Ltd, Harmondsworth,
Middlesex, England
Penguin Books Inc., 7110 Ambassador Road,
Baltimore, Maryland 21207, U.S.A.
Penguin Books Australia Ltd., Ringwood,
Victoria, Australia

The translations of *Juan Ramón Jiménez: Fifty Spanish Poems* first published in England by
The Dolphin Book Company, Oxford, 1950
The translations of *Castilian Ilexes: Versions from Antonio Machado* first published in England by
Oxford University Press, 1963
Published in Penguin Books 1974

Made and printed in Great Britain by
Richard Clay (The Chaucer Press) Ltd
Set in Monotype Bembo

Contents

Acknowledgement

The publishers and the editor of this volume gratefully acknowledge the most generous assistance given by J. L. Gili in preparing this version of Juan Ramón Jiménez's translations and in revising the Introduction by the late J. B. Trend.

Juan Ramón Jiménez

Translated by J. B. Trend and J. L. Gili
with an Introduction by J. B. Trend

Introduction

Contemporary poetry in Spanish began to attract general attention only with the Civil War of 1936–9 and the murder of Federico García Lorca. The result has been a tendency to take Lorca for the only Spanish poet of his time, though he was in fact a younger member of a brilliant school and a flourishing modern tradition, represented in other fields by the well-known names of Falla, Casals and Picasso. In Spanish poetry today, the central figure is Juan Ramón Jiménez. The poets, like the musicians and the painters, were scattered by the Civil War and the persecution which followed it. Antonio Machado died of pneumonia in the Pyrenees, escaping in midwinter from Barcelona; Miguel Hernández died of consumption in prison.

All the poets of that school, and all the writers who were their friends, were descended from the Spanish and Spanish-American *modernistas* of 1898; but they had grown out of the original *modernismo* and were reacting against it. For *modernismo*, in spite of its name (or because of it), had dated; and by 1928 there was little of it left beyond its effect on the technique of writing Spanish verse. This poetry could not fail to be affected by the Symbolists. One of the chief symbols had been the swan – the swan of Baudelaire and Verlaine and Yeats. But Juan Ramón Jiménez once remarked that the swan on dry land is a goose; and in the end it was a Mexican poet, Enrique González Martínez, who – remembering Verlaine and what he had said about rhetoric – called on all Spanish-speaking poets to wring the swan's neck, although he did so in a sonnet of those alexandrines which owed their form to Rubén Darío, the chief poet in Spanish of the swan whose neck he was wringing.

All the tendencies of *modernismo* – the new things the poets were saying and the new forms in which they were saying them – are to be found in the poetry of Rubén Darío, who was born in the Central American republic of Nicaragua but eventually became the most cosmopolitan poet who had ever written in Spanish. Some of the forms, and verses of much the same kind, had been used in Spanish-speaking America before: by Gutiérrez Nájera in Mexico, by José Asunción Silva in Colombia, and by Julio del Casal in Cuba; while an earlier, romantic Argentine poet, Esteban Echeverría, has an occasional line which sounds more modern than anything to be heard at that time in Spain. There were also stirrings in Spain itself towards the end of the century: that delicate, premature child of French symbolism, Gustavo Adolfo Bécquer, and another Andaluz, Salvador Rueda, each in his own way looked forward to the new poetry of the end of the century; while there was something of the same feeling in the clear Catalan poems of Jacint Verdaguer and the misty Celtic longing of Rosalía de Castro, whether she wrote in ringing Castilian Spanish or in her own wistful, Galician dialect of Portuguese.

Many of the ideas of the new poetry, if not the forms, were there in the rough-hewn verses of Unamuno. Unamuno was inclined to write poetry – and in particular sonnets – as if he were heaving a brick at a wall, writing verse, as Keats once said, 'with all its lines abrupt and angular'. But in the end it was Unamuno the thinker, even more than Rubén Darío the prosodist – *modernismo ideal* rather than *modernismo formal* – who raised the stale, conventional poetry of the Spanish nineteenth century to the level it had reached in 1935. The effects, the convergence of

'Unamuno within and Rubén Darío without', were at once apparent in Antonio Machado. Juan Ramón Jiménez, who knew Machado well, has spoken of the strong influence on Machado at that time of certain poems of Rubén Darío, and of that northern corner of Madrid, where the first University College was afterwards built, the *Residencia de Estudiantes* with which they were both to be so closely connected.

The second wave came in the 1920s, when the younger poets looked back, and up, to Góngora, Garcilaso and Gil Vicente, the three sixteenth-century masters whose *Renascence* technique and humanist thought had tightened up the tension of Spanish poetry to make it a satisfactory modern instrument. Meanwhile, the still small voice of Bécquer continued to be heard by really sensitive poetic natures. Antonio Machado heard it in the winding *Galerías* of his own mind; and Juan Ramón Jiménez heard it while, with his fine poetic sensibility, his keen eye, his alert ear and his strangely beautiful handwriting, he continued the new movement in Spanish poetry and eventually spread it to all the twenty countries where Spanish is spoken.

Juan Ramón Jiménez, born in 1881, was already publishing poems by 1898. For him, *modernismo* was part of the general movement for freedom from romanticism – literary, artistic, scientific, social and religious – which had begun in Spain and Spanish-speaking America at about the same time. In Spain the movement of thought and feeling owed much to the teaching, encouragement and friendliness of Don Francisco Giner de los Ríos at the 'Free School', the *Institución Libre de Enseñanza*, and the University college, the *Residencia de Estudiantes*. It is surprising how many of the later poets have been connected with these institutions.

Juan Ramón Jiménez worked at poetry consistently throughout his life, either writing new poems or polishing and refining poems already published. He did many of the things also done by his Spanish contemporaries, but did them first.

'Spain', Jiménez has said, 'is a country which, taken all in all, is deeply realist and falsely religious, Catholic rather than Christian, ecclesiastical rather than spiritual, a country of roots and feet rather than of wings; and the true poetry of Spain, the only possible kind of written lyric poetry, was begun by the feelings of Everyman (*el sentir del pueblo*) and by the few strange mystics, whose landscape was the sullen rock and the marvellous sky. They all try to fly, naturally; and for that reason the best Spanish lyrics have been, and are, inevitably mystical, with God or without Him; for the poet is a mystic, though he does not necessarily have a god.'

In his early period Jiménez concentrated on the description of objects by enrichment, not economy: by crowded sensations and by words consciously poetic and chosen, as in the wonderful evocation of a cathedral in the south of Spain, 'Cathedral in a Country Town'. The rather elegiac mood of these poems was sometimes relieved by satire, though that too was presented in the same elegiac metre. The satires were called *poesías al revés*, poems inside out. These have often been overlooked although they are an important part of his character and work. Jiménez, from copying or describing what he saw, or allowing its existence to be deduced from what he said, soon came to occupy himself not with objects but with the way light fell upon them. In this he was following the familiar road of the painters – he too had once thought of being a painter – who have passed from painting objects to painting light itself. The poem 'Last Light' combines this pictorial technique with an exquisite, dancing movement of the lines. The English version given here is a clumsy imitation; but it may show how the original was meant to go, in the way that R. C. Trevelyan's translations of Greek choruses show the movement of the original Greek.

It is not true that 'poems that are written in one language can only be enjoyed by a particular race or nationality'. Such poems are not poems in any true sense; for the genuine quality of poetry does not depend on the language in which it is written. The object of a translation from Juan Ramón Jiménez should not be to produce a second-hand poem in English on the same subject, but to convey in English the exotic impression of the original poem in Spanish. The translation, Trevelyan says, should be 'disinfected' from all English associations. A poem is bound to lose much in translation; Cervantes said that it was like looking at the wrong side of a tapestry. But sometimes – in Arthur Waley's translations from the Chinese classics, and Harold Acton's versions from Chinese contemporaries – translation can be made very well worth while, even allowing that a large proportion of the total effect of the poem will, to any one who can understand it in its own language, appear to be lost.

This seems particularly true of Jiménez's *Sonetos espirituales*, written in 1914–15. In an English version the rhymes must often be sacrificed; that was the poet's own method, he tells us, in translating Samain and Moréas into Spanish; for even if it were possible to produce a rhymed version of reasonable accuracy, the rhyming sounds would have no relation to the rhymes of the original. Spanish is believed to be an 'easy' language; but the scientific, phonetic fact remains that not *one* of the Spanish sounds is exactly the same as the corresponding sound in English. Yet the rhythm and movement of the language can be imitated, and something recognizable will be carried over in a translation. Poetry does not really depend on the colour or vowel-harmony or beauty of the original verbal sounds, but on the colour of the poetic emotions; and in most modern poetry the nuance of the poetic emotions is more important than the nuance of the words. Rhyme and regularity, a Chinese poet told Harold Acton, may not only be disadvantageous to poetic emotion; they may distort it. But the movement, one may add, is something permanent.

One of the sonnets, 'The Poet to His Soul', looks forward to Heidegger and Sartre. But Spaniards do not need Heidegger to make them existentialists; that outlook – or what is essential in that outlook – is theirs by nature, and without conscious strain. This particular sonnet is near to the later Antonio Machado; but here again Jiménez was first. It is unnecessary to look at it through the spectacles of dogmatic theology or describe it in the jargon of modern mysticism; for it expresses something fundamentally Spanish: a feeling which all genuine Spaniards have somewhere within them – the threat of the ineluctable, felt so strongly by Unamuno.

In form, the *Sonetos espirituales* revive the direct inspiration of the Spanish sonneteers of the sixteenth century, without the complication of the seventeenth or the bombast of the nineteenth; they have no surprise in store in the last verse, nor any unusual rhymes. But Jiménez was seeking a simpler form of expression. Alexandrines and hendecasyllables seemed too 'baroque'; and among a good deal of poetry in prose, he wrote the marvellous prose-study *Platero y yo*, published in 1914. Platero (the name means, literally, 'silversmith') was the poet's donkey. In those days there were few cars in those parts. People in the South of Spain habitually rode on donkeys, and looked after them like Sancho Panza looking after his *rucio*, Dapple. Yet the principal character is neither Platero nor Juan Ramón; it is the whole population of a white, gleaming town in Andalucia: Moguer, the poet's birthplace, one of those small seaports from which the caravels of Columbus set out for China and discovered America.

Jiménez had been reading Yeats, 'A.E.', and Blake, and translating Synge's *Riders to the Sea*; but the poems written in 1915 and published in *Estio* (Summer) were not influenced by the Anglo-Irish poets, or by his future wife's attractive Spanish versions of Rabindranath Tagore. They show him, however, experimenting in free verse – or rather, verses of different length following one another irregularly, for it is difficult to find a line of Jiménez which is not a genuine Spanish verse of some kind. He abandoned rhyme, and fell back on the traditional Spanish assonance which Spanish poets have been using continuously for eight hundred years.

Next came a visit to America, and a happy marriage. America in itself had little outward effect on Jiménez. There was no violent reaction in his poetry, as there was later with García Lorca. The chief effects were made by the Atlantic crossings, and the *Diario de un poeta recién casado*, in verse and prose, is mainly a book of the sea. New York, though it did not have the effect on him that it had on other Spanish poets, was nevertheless the inspiration of one of his finest poems, dedicated to Antonio Machado. There is a good poem, too, on New York harbour, dedicated to the memory of Enrique and Amparo Granados, the brilliant composer and his wife, who had left New York not long before and were on board the *Sussex* when she was torpedoed in mid-channel. It is dated 'New York, at my window in 11th Street, 27 March, 1916, before dawn and in yellow moonlight'.

The time came for packing up and returning to Spain, and in 'an empty room with trunks all fastened, 6th June (night) 1916', Jiménez wrote his poem of farewell,

'Remorse'. The voyage back began with two difficult and puzzling poems: 'Convexities' and 'Rose of the Sea'; but by 15 June he was at work on an important poem, 'Departure', of which he afterwards made an admirable gramophone record for the *Centro de Estudios Históricos* at Madrid. It was so far his longest and most ambitious single poem, but was followed by several collections of shorter poems: *Eternidades*, for instance, published in 1916–17, and *Piedra y cielo* (Rock and sky), 1917–18.

What kind of poetry ought one to pursue? Not 'pure' poetry, whatever that was. Hence Jiménez regarded the quest for pure poetry as a wrong road, like that pseudo-religious pride in self-abasement, squalor and an unwashed body which had so great an influence on the poetry of Verlaine and Rimbaud. Poetry was a state of mind, the Symbolists said: *de l'âme pour l'âme, résumant tout, parfums, sons, couleurs*; poetry should not be pure, but naked. The bare precision of the word, faithful to the absolute precision of the thought; something, Yeats said,

> Where passion and precision have been one.

In 1922 Jiménez published *Segunda Antolojía Poética (1898–1918)*, a revision of the book he had published in New York in 1919. The volumes called *Poesía (en verso)* and *Belleza*, in which he showed himself alert to the newest tendencies in the poetry of the time, were published in 1924. From then until 1936, the flow of limited and privately-printed editions continued. *Poesía y prosa*, a selection for children – of all ages – appeared in 1934, and *Canción*, a collection of many new poems and revisions of earlier ones, in the summer of 1936.

On the outbreak of Civil War he remained in Madrid, making himself useful in whatever ways he could, and in particular collecting homeless children from the streets and reading to them in his own flat. But when the time came for all those to leave Madrid whose presence there was not strictly necessary, he went to America, living for a time in Havana and then in Florida. Some poems have undoubtedly been lost, and the manuscripts of others stolen; but a reprint of the *Segunda Antolojía* appeared in Buenos Aires in 1944 and a new collection, *La estación total, con las Canciones de la nueva luz*, in 1946.

In *Poesía (en verso)* and *Belleza*, Jiménez was seeking poetry in new places, 'the beauty that's undesigned and tardy – always there for the improvident'; in the no-man's-land of 'Dawn Outside the Walls', for instance. 'Peace', however, is a strangely moving and beautiful poem; while 'Rose of the Shadow', and above all the first of the two poems called 'Pact', represent his original and highly individual genius at one of its highest points. They had appeared in various anthologies, particularly in the fine collection of contemporary Spanish poetry edited by Gerardo Diego, *Poesía española, 1915–31*, but were only collected by the poet himself in *La estación total* in 1946.

The last anthology of his work, *Tercera Antolojía Poética*, was published in 1957. This includes his latest poems, charged with metaphysical content, such as those published in *Animal de Fondo*, from which comes the last poem in the present selection.

In 1956 the Swedish Academy awarded him the Nobel Prize for Literature for his 'lyrical poetry which in the Spanish language sets an example of high spiritual quality and artistic purity'.

Jiménez also published admirable prose. Not only *Platero y yo*, which has gone into several editions in several different countries, but newer prose, unlike anything which had been written in Spanish before. The pieces were collected and published in Buenos Aires in 1942: *Españoles de tres mundos*. They are portraits of Spanish people, composed over a long period of years; but among them the portraits which remain most in the memory are those of Don Francisco Giner and Don Manuel Cossío.

For nearly twenty-five years Juan Ramón Jiménez had lived in Madrid for preference; the *andaluz* of Andalucia had become the *andaluz universal*. Though he demanded peace and quite in his own house, he could tolerate the bleating taxi-cabs of the *Centro* of Madrid which drove an English acquaintance to distraction. '*El rebaño*', he remarked: 'the herd'; and the English acquaintance caught a vision, not only of Don Quixote and the armies which were sheep, but of all the ages of Castile, with the migratory shepherds and vast herds of lowing cattle of the Mesta, jostling one another along a *cañada real*.

J. B. TREND

Green

Green was the maiden, green, green!
Green her eyes were, green her hair.

The wild rose in her green wood
was neither red nor white, but green.

Through the green air she came.
(The whole earth turned green for her).

The shining gauze of her garment
was neither blue nor white, but green.

Over the green sea she came.
(And even the sky turned green then).

My life will always leave unlatched
a small green gate to let her in.

Francina's Garden

With dripping bunches of lilac
I splashed her over the shoulder,
and over her fair white form
the jewels rolled in clear round dew-drops.

Oh, fly away, drenched and glistening,
over the beaded sand!

(The flesh would turn pale and wither
though the roses still were red,
pale as a silver apple
that dawn had dusted with hoar-frost).

She fled me, away from the water,
while the roses still were red.
And she laughed, mischievous.
Her laughter itself was water.

With rods of lilac and water,
even as she ran, I beat her.

Southern Sea

In the deep blue and fevered lethargy of the siesta
the garden flames in the sun. A smell of burnt roses.
The tide heaves between the unmoving leafy garlands:
a million million diamonds gleaming from sunny waves.

Amber cupolas and towers take fire in the far distance
in an oceanic city of veiled fantasy:
leaping, laughing and twinkling; momentary reflections
of gleaming tiles, of bronzes, of rows of crystal panes.

The water spreads out its cool silver fans
to the green calm of hushed leaves;
and through the solitary silence moves a frigate:
white, with swelling sails, among the rocks of flame.

Winter Scene: Snow

Where, oh where have they hidden all the colours
on this wan day of white and black?
The foliage, black; the water, grey; the earth
and sky, an ashen blackness;
and the dejected city
only an old romantic etching.

Men on the road are black;
black, the frightened bird
that darts across the garden like an arrow.
Even the silence is hard and colourless.

The evening falls. The sky
has nothing of kindliness. And now at sunset
a livid yellow gleam, hardly resplendent,
or hardly a gleam at all. Out in the country,
all rust-red iron.
Night comes on like a funeral.
Everything is draped in mourning,
and all is cold; no stars at all, but white
and black, just as the day is: white and black.

Island

Oh, for a solitude as pure
as a fall of snow!
A whiteness all divine, unanimous:
a silence that is permanent.

I wish everyone far away!
Oh, that I might not remember
even myself! The ideal alone:
a fountain and an avenue.

The fountain will not be playing;
but in timeless ecstasy,
like a diamond reflecting
a vast, unending sunset;
a sunset that will never open
on flaming, tropical gardens,
but will be a fantasy
all in indelible white.

Let everyone leave me alone.
I myself shall not remember.
. . . A peace, gentler, and more delicate
than a fall of snow.

Cathedral in a Country Town

Cathedral far in the south in the summer wheat fields,
where the hard sunshine is honey to rose-windows,
open to all the bees of magical, dreaming sunsets,
a honeycomb of colour in soft maternal stone-work.

Forgetfulness, drowsy and pure, idealizing
flaming pinnacles, halos of burnished gold,
where sluggish bells, made eternal
by their clear blindness, speak of time past.

This quiet country, winding river and well-stocked
    garden,
never so good, as seen from the top of the burning
    tower;
and there too the cheerful breezes, meeting among the
    bell-strokes,
are clashes of new light . . .
                                        And salty, sea-borne visions,
roads to a new glory, leading away to twilight
of fragrance and silence, down in the quiet corners
where discoloured, golden pieces of architecture,
ancient ruins of fallen skies, are hidden away.

Was It a Smooth Stream

Was it a smooth stream, a sheet of paper, my forehead
reflected, smoothed out all the words,
vibrating through their heavens like the voices of stars
lost in a labyrinth of bell-notes?

Notes that were slowly forming, light on light, sound
on sound,
rose upon rose, tear upon tear;
some strange structure, blazing with light and singing,
mellowed by moonlight in my soul.

Endless end of a broken and nameless harmony,
never in thought to be extinguished;
those dry leaves, the flash of a crystal, one lone blossom,
deep in the shadow intermingled.

Some unknown thing from afar, that reaches down to
our life here,
by winding ways of transfiguration,
like a shooting-star trailing pollen of silver
across the skies of dream.

Storm

The light is a running curtain of sunsets, shuffled
together,
down in the dripping street on a rainy afternoon.
But then all changes. The clear sky is suddenly darkened,
or else the dark becomes clear.

There is a livid music
of silver that's out of tune, instead of the splendid sound,
the golden harmony of the celestial tubas;
great chimerical organs, bright with melodious embers
of clear-skied sunsets which never have an end.

Misery and proximity. The black revolution
in heaven throws monstrous heaps of flesh on to our
beaches.
Upheavals of flesh and spirit, disorders at high altitudes,
lead us in drunken terror to gusts of real madness.

Who Knows . . .

Who knows what's at the back of every minute!
How many times the sunrise
has happened behind a mountain!
How often the royal thrill of a new horizon
held in its golden womb a clap of thunder!
That rose was deadly poison.
That cruel sword gave life.
I dreamed of a flowery meadow
– at the far end of a long road –
I found myself in a marsh.
Then I dreamed of the glory of all things human,
and found myself in the divine.

Lightness

My window-curtain,
in the majestic stillness and the silence
of the unruffled early morning,
moving softly to light breezes.

Oh, lovely moment
that makes the living brother to the dead,
one like another (there's no telling
which is the dead and which the living)
in the one great intensity of breathing!
. . . All the world must be dead now, or else all
living still.

And those light breezes of the early morning
move the white, waving curtain
of my wide-open window . . .

I think
this gentle movement of my curtain
is the life of the universe, all the breath
of the earth, all the strength
remaining with us
of earth's primeval impetus, the light sound
of its whirling, heavenly orbit.

And the curtain's
moving now,
in the light breezes of the early morning,
all white . . .

Oh, how full is the least thing
that fills the world, and fixes
the boundless contemplation
of such uncertainty: the leaf
that falls, the drop
that sparkles,
the scent that passes . . .!

And the curtain
that's blue now and not white
– for the night is ended,
While I watch its swaying uncertainty –
is moving softly, still, in the light breeze.

The Great Voice

Nothing troubling our peace; only a bell and a bird
singing . . .
It may be both of them are speaking with the sunset.

The silence is pure gold. The nightfall clear crystal.
A pure roving breath is swaying the cool trees.
And, far away from all else, a limpid brook is running,
dividing pearl from pearl in its flight to eternity.

Solitude! Solitude! Everything clear and hushed now
Nothing troubling our peace; only a bell and a bird
singing . . .
But love lives far off, serene and indifferent;
the fond heart is free yet, and knows no joy or sorrow.
Colours giving it pleasure: a breeze, a touch, a sweet
scent.
It swims on a calm lake immune from sentiment.

Nothing troubling our peace; only a bell and a bird
singing . . .
To hold eternity in the palm of my hand!

Last Light

Light, with the wood in shadow, are you lost then?
The sun is down, light, with the wood in shadow!
Look, light, you are left alone
to play, there, with the leaves so green.
What will you do, now that your sun's left you alone?

. . . Come to this leaf of paper,
this white leaf and my dark sorrow.
Oh, rosy-fingered one, make gold for me forever!

The Sword of the Spirit

How trustfully you lie there
under my eyes, but eluding
the spirit's hold: your fragile
fairy loveliness in contact
with my body, all unfettered,
that every instinct would stir!

(You yield yourself like death).

Delicate white lily,
transplanted happily –
to flowery fields of heaven!
The solemnity of slumber
makes you (your power a portent),
a keen-edged sword at my side.

Nothing

To your abandonment I have opposed
my godlike tower of intelligence.
I climb up there; my blood-stained heart has caused
the sea to be empurpled with its sense.

I'll manufacture dawn from my own shadow,
protect my lyre from vain and wanton winds,
search in my self for my own sustenance; . . .
but, ah, if that sweet peace should bring me nothing!

Nothing, yes, nothing, nothing! Oh that the waters
might now receive my soul; and in this manner
the world be one great prison, chill and naught!

For you are you; you are the human spring,
of earth, air, water, fire – of everything;
while I myself am nothing but my thought.

Diana

The wood, when your footstep whitens it,
becomes a backcloth for your human peace,
the great reason for your innocent escape,
and whose serenity your clear flight exalts.

The light of that prodigious day turned brighter,
the time it shone on your shoulder. The whole morning
came in your wake. For you, the streams were running
faster; the breeze with you came fresher, lighter.

I thought when I saw you in the wood so green,
pagan and proud, a-hunting you would ride;
yet you were both the hunted and hunter too.

Fleeing, but from yourself: pursuing . . . but then
you were hunting yourself, Diana wild,
with no more point or passion than the dawn.

The Poet to His Soul

Day after day you keep the branch protected
in case the rose may come; you go alert
day after day, your ear warm at the gate
of your body, for the arrow unexpected.

No wave of thought can flow from non-existence
and not derive, from your receptive shade,
the larger gleam. All night, you are awake
in your particular star, to life's persistence.

On things you leave indelible impresses;
then, turned to an afterglow upon the height,
revive in things whereon your seal is set.

Your rose shall be the pattern of all roses;
your ear, of harmony; of every light
your thought; of every waking star, your state.

Summer Time

Once I put-on the time of my heart,
just as it were a watch,
set to a calmer moment.

Happiness never came near me;
my happiness stayed as it was,
unaffected by the trick;
never, never was on time!

And reality, confused,
lived by the hour that was past:
the hour of my deep despair.

And so, wearily, I put back
your hands again, O restless heart.

Nothing More?

Only my face and the sky;
there's no other universe!
My face, alone, and the sky!

– Between them, the wind blows pure:
a fond caress, the only hand
that brings plenitude of joy:
the wind ever rising and falling –

Above me, all that has life;
all the dream I feel within me,
peopling my sense with wings
of the dream-sent harmony.

Nothing more.
Are you, perchance,
are you the wind that comes and goes,
the wind of heaven, love, on my face?

How Near My Soul Already

How near my soul already
what is so immensely far away
and still out of reach!
Like the light of a star;
like the unnamed voice
brought by a dream; like the passing-by
of a rider in the distance
when heard by breathless listener
with ear bent to the ground;
like the sea on the telephone . . .

Life's made like that
inside us, with the unextinguished light
of a day of pure enjoyment
that still shines elsewhere.

Oh, how sweet, how sweet;
truth not yet real, how sweet!

Nocturne

The sea provides no well-known waves,
no stations, halts or stopping-places;
water and moon, no more, night after night!

My thought flies to the land,
that, although alien, was one's own
when crossing it in the night of trains,
through the same old places, at the same
time as before . . .
– Distant mother,
sleeping land,
with strong steadfast arms,
a constant quiet refuge
– tomb of eternal life
with the same ornament renewed –;
mother-land, always
waiting in its unique
truth for the sad look
in the wanderer's eyes!

My thought flies to the land
– olive-groves at daybreak –,
immutable under the white,
yellow or rose-red moon,
always awaiting the return
of those who, neither belonging nor possessing,
loved her always.

Sky

I had forgotten you,
sky, and you were nothing
more than a vague presence of light,
seen – without a name –
by my tired indolent eyes.
And you appeared, among the lazy
and despairing words of the traveller,
as a vision of small repeated pools
in a watery landscape seen in a dream . . .

Today I have gazed at you slowly,
and you have gradually risen up to your name.

Nocturne

To Antonio Machado

This is celestial geometry:
an old astrologer's planning
for a great and tall city – towers
black-lined, fine-drawn, tapering, all his own –

As if, from an ultimate balcony,
all lay under the keen eye
of the astrologer.
Aspect,
ascendent, mansion and conjunction,
with every secret open and released
in the diaphanous atmosphere
of this profound deep blue transparency.

What sudden blaze, what menace,
what positions, what portents,
in the imminent certainty
of the exceptional truth! Anatomy
of starry heaven, the science
of their function, for us and for themselves.

A piercing cry, immense and lonely;
lone as a wandering star. –

. . . How far off, now,
from those who once were us,
in our long distant springtime, on that evening
– in Washington Square, so calm and tranquil –
who dreamed such dreams and loved with such great
love.

Smoke and Gold

To Enrique and Amparo Granados

So much sea in the yellow moonlight
lying between us, Spain! And so much sea tomorrow
in early morning sunshine . . .
. . . Sailing
in the wan light of daybreak, dim-seen ships
sounding their mournful sirens, naked visions;
sleepless, I hear them take farewell.
– In solitary splendour
the moon, oh, shade of Poe! dies over Broadway –
Sleepless, I hear them, my forehead pressing
against the rigid panes; I hear them
take farewell, once and again, amid their dreams . . .
– and now the daybreak is nothing but an empty space
in the frigid light where only yesterday
the jet-black mole was glowing –
dreams in the dream of all of those now sleeping
in that part of their life that is still living
side by side
with that part of their life already dead.

How far off, oh! how far off
from you and from me, – and from all things
– olive-groves at daybreak – ,
When I hear the alert given – Death! –
breaking into the harmony of my spirit
– immeasurable sea of joy and sorrow –
in the yellow light
of that sinking solitary moon, Spain!

(*New York, at my window in 11th Street, 27 March, 1916, before dawn and in yellow moonlight.*)

Remorse

Soon time will cover it
with roses, that there may be
no remembrance.

The roses will be different
with an unpredicted magic,
covering every lonely hour with gold
or shadow –
moment propitious for tragic memories.

And there among the fairest
and gayest
of climbing, rambling roses, white and crimson,
that leave the past no opportunity,
the body will once more
be twined about
the spirit.

(*New York, empty room with trunks all fastened,
6 June, night, 1916.*)

Convexities

The sky had its back towards me;
the sea also turned its back, and between their naked
    shoulders,
the day rebounded from my shoulders too.

All that the day had left
was that which all had said before.
Are not our three bosoms open wide,
facing the all of all men,
the all which all refuse to know
of everything!

Rose of the Sea

The moon has taken the sea from the sea
and given it back to the sea. By her rare beauty,
and by her tranquil and virginal surrender,
making truth appear to be truth no longer,
feigning a truth eternal and universal
from one that is not so.
                    Yes.
                              Divine simplicity:
to defeat the known and fill with a new spirit
the old and tried truth.
A rose that was unforeseen, and takes away
the rose from the rose itself, but then gives back
to the rose a rose.

Departure

Before those pure unblemished nights at sea, my spirit,
more lonely now than ever, had not known
that eagerness upon the day appointed
to sail out none knew whither.

This is the gate
to the pathway lighted on the sea by moonbeams
with all their centuries of loveliness,
of chastity, of whiteness, peace and grace;
sick with longing for the absent movement
of waves now stilled.

A seething spring
and the ghosts of white lilies; a soft melody,
a heavenly sound made music in the crystal drops of spray
of wavelets toppling their translucent crests
with every colour that the rainbow matched,
with a tantalizing savour of deliciousness;
life was ecstasy then, till all was over.

Magic and pleasure; and more, there in the shadow
where certain strange bright eyes were ever burning;
more than the vision of that long-chanted love,
simple and sure and true as steel,
that love we hardly hope to find – so truly
it seemed to us a dream of far-off ages.

Yet thus it was, and thus began
our love, and in that manner I beheld it
with childish heart, when, open
like roses, my eyes
raised their glance all black from those white towers,
white in the iris of my dreamland,
to the lofty clarity of a paradise.

Even so, that petal fallen from the sky,
where, wrapped within my soul, it lay –
(like any other, it was; separate and free).
So it was, and so it is now; and thence it passed
through smooth-cut galleries of infallible
architecture, of water, earth, fire and air,
like this unending night, I know not whither,
led by the unfailing light of a few stars.
Even so there came the beginning without end – the
morning
of the desire of the spirit,
to fly out by the door, away to her unknown centre.

Oh, original whiteness, for ever
first!
Marmoreal reality of the blind white light!
Unique rapturous whiteness!
. . . The whiteness of this night, the sea, the moon!

Nocturne

The ship, both slow and fast at once, outruns the water
but not the sky.
The blue remains behind, opening to burnished silver,
with blue in front once more.
The mast swings to and fro, returning always
– like the big hand to the same hour
on the clock-face –
to the same stars as before;
hour after hour in sable and green.
The body's left to dreaming
of the world that is his, of the other world too
that is not his. The soul remains and follows.
ever in search of her long dominion.

Intelligence . . .

Intelligence, oh give me
the proper name for everything.
. . . So that my word be truly
the thing in itself,
created expressly for me by my soul.
That they follow my footsteps
all who have never known the nature of things;
that they follow my footsteps
all who have forgotten the nature of things;
that they follow, too, my footsteps
even they who have loved all things for themselves.
Intelligence, oh give me
the proper name, and *your* name,
and theirs and mine, for all things.

Maiden, at First She Met Me

Maiden, at first she met me
all clothed in innocence,
and I loved her like a child.
Then she was dressing up
in goodness knows what fancies;
I hated her, not knowing why.
She even became a queen,
magnificent in her treasures . . .
what gall and bitterness, and oh, what nonsense!
. . . Then she began undressing,
and I could smile upon her.
Soon she was left in her shift,
in her former innocence;
I believed in her once more.
Then she took off even that
and appeared before me naked . . .
Oh, passion of all my life! Oh, poetry,
naked and mine forever!

Aurora

Daybreak brings along with it
that sad feeling of arrival
by train, at a railway station that isn't one's own.

How harshly sound the voices,
of a day one knows is merely transitory.
– oh, my dear life!

– Up there, now, with the daybreak a child's crying . . .

To Dante

Yours the sonnet, the likeness
of a fair woman chaste and naked
who took me on her knees and held me,
embracing me with celestial embraces.

And then I dreamed of it, and of her.
                                        There was a fountain,
and two arching jets were spouting into a basin
above me, and then poured out their thin streams
into two other basins.

The Poem

I plucked the whole plant, root and leaves,
dripping still with the dew of early morning.

Oh, how it watered the earth,
everywhere scented and moistened;
what raindrops, what a blinding fall of stars,
on my face, in my eyes!

How Immense and Ragged . . .

How immense and ragged the rent,
torn in my life and in all things,
that I may be with all myself
in everything;
and that I never cease to be
with all myself in everything!

Memory

Oh, memories in secret,
far off the winding pathways
of all my other memories!

The thought that in the night time
unlooked-for comes again,
strange as a wild rose in the desert,
strange as a star that shines at noonday,
– the agony of cold forgetting –
the rod and staff of all
that is most worth living,
the life scarce lived at all!
                                        Always
the path is dull, arid;
then the miracle happens,
the only true springtime,
of all the memories once forgotten!

Memory

A stream is flowing in the depths
of my spirit, undermining me.
I can hardly maintain
my strength. No help comes to me
from heaven. Even stars
deceive me; none are there
above me, only below me, down in the depths . . .

Am I? I *shall* be!
I shall be – turned to a ripple
on the stream of memory . . .

With you, flowing water!

After Many Years

If only the memory
you have of me were this blue vault of heaven
in May-time, hung all over
with the pure, shining stars of all my actions!

If my acts had been equal, as the stars are, all unsullied;
limpid, good and tranquil, like the stars in their courses!

– And there I see you smiling in your dreams,
dreams that are all your memories of my life! –

Hill-Top

The enormous almond in flower!
White to the top, in the great, full silence of white
moonlight;
the trunk all black in the total peace of the dark shadow.
So while I climbed up by the steep rock to you,
I thought that you plunged your great trunk
right to the depths of my being,
and starred the whole of heaven with my soul.

Seas

I felt that my little boat
had run aground, and in the depths
lay some large object.
                                        And nothing
had happened? Nothing . . . All still . . . Rollers . . .

Nothing had happened? Or was it that everything
                                                                        had happened,
and we had come gently into a new world?

Epitaph on an Unknown Sailor

Look not on earth, you who would find
your grave, but in the firmament.
– It was a star rained death on you.
The stone shall not lie heavy; it is a universe
of dream-stuff. –
In nescientness you dwell:
in all – in heaven, at sea, on earth – a dead man.

The Boat Comes In . . .

The boat comes in, obscure and black,
into the transparent blackness
of the immense harbour.
                                        Peace and cold.
                                            – Those who are waiting,
still asleep in their dream,
warm inside themselves yet motionless and distant
     within it;
from here, perhaps . . .

  Oh, our very real vigil, beside the dream
of doubt in others! Certainty, next to
the dream anxious for us! –

                                     Peace. Silence.
Silence that, on breaking with the dawn,
will speak in another way.

Fritillary! Light!

Fritillary! Light!
But the beauty is gone when I arrive
at her rose.

Blindly, blindly pursue her . . .
Half catch her here, half catch her there . . .

All that's left in my hand:
the form of her flight!

Before the Virgin Shadow

Perpetual penetration,
perpetual virginity –
shadow! Even as on that day
when first I came to see you
demanding of you your secret,
weighed down with boundless passion.

Virgin dark and mysterious,
stained to the iris depths
that are scarce to be seen; all
black, with the sublimity
of stars that ever strive
up there, to find you here on earth.

Dawn Outside the Walls

Everything bare and uncovered, all white –
lime, nightmare, adobe, anaemia, cold –
facing the east. How close it is to life;
how hard the life is, too! An animal likeness
as touching the body – the root, the scoriae –
the soul still badly situated –
a likeness mineral and vegetable!
Sun striking down on men,
on pigs, on cabbage-stalks, on mud walls!
How false your gaiety, that are so lonely;
lonely in time, perhaps, not in the soul.

The whole sky is enclosed
by steaming damp mounds
of the dung-heaped horizon.
Here and there, sweepings
of the night. Slices
of green moon half eaten,
glass splinters of false stars;
wall-paper stripped off the blue sky,
with the plaster still fresh. The birds
still barely awake, in the crude white moonlight,
a street-lamp almost out.
Strange collection of things and people!
A sadness that is genuine, because so lonely;
lonely in soul, you'd say, but not in time.

Figuration

Oh, days that lend their colour to the night:
the daybreak – golden dahlias dripped with dew –
the tunnel's end of dream;
the zenith – magic ceiling wrapped in flames –
from the cavern of deep sleep;
– a golden pheasant in the crimson sunset –
a red sky from the prison-house of day-dreams:
– the beauty that's undesigned and tardy, always
there for the improvident,
there for the slovenly: the only kind of life!

Peace

When at daybreak
the campanulas unfold
their red flowers to the moon,
you will not be at home then,
naked white shadow.

– You will be serenely
at rest and smiling
surrounded by new happiness,
contented with your lot
that makes you indifferent,
since life is followed by death. –

The day will kindle,
with most melancholy light;
the green and cold breeze
will pour, like rain-water,
onto the empty terraced-roof.

. . . And one will get up,
and race unwillingly through the morning chores,
and unwillingly see and hear in every corner
the shouts, the running to and fro, the bragging
– sun on the poor defenceless flesh and blood –,
the dazzling light of bitter ugliness.

Balcony in Autumn

Out on the long wire of the telephone
a large star quivers, a green dragon-fly.
The town, now autumn's here again,
becomes a new place. Breezes
pencil the outlines of the roofs
– the telegraph-poles, the lightning-conductors, the
lines and clothes-props –
seen in a sunset of deep transparency.

– Woman and cat lean out
from a parapet (cage, boat's bridge?, no, a roof garden!),
their silhouettes
cut equal and black. –

That's right! Both hands
back in our pockets already. Delightful! How endless
are the varieties offered again and again
to the human soul transplanted to new pastures.

Now the town swings, is afloat, weighs anchor.
The whole world off to sea? God is a sailor?

Borne along by the moment
by ship or car or train or aeroplane,
all things running, vibrating, turning, flying –
to new harbours and new parks and new mountains
and new cities in thousands.

Out of the window open wide
what great perspective, ah!
vicarious eternity!

Pact

The Guadarrama comes out of the night
a bluer blue, a redder rose;
stands there all bathed in bare infinities,
in light and pattern
of incalculable eternity.

Not yet is it ours, nor has it come again;
but still in the deep-toned wind it lies apart
and out of touch with us;
nor has it reached us on the normal scale,
to plant itself on the earth,
and still is formed of material of other nature.

Let it stand forth for surety
to that unclimbed surface
of our well-known familiar reality,
when all its ways and all its waters
have found their point of fusion gone in darkness;
then this damp theatre
of house-fronts taken unaware by daylight,
coverings for horizontal flesh,
will be Madrid in Spain; this tattered rag,
faded red and faded yellow,
on top of a box, a row of empty partitions,
– homes for men and for women –
this thing will be our national flag . . . For
after all,
we can only be what we are.

So another day will begin,
vaguely conscious of duty to be done,
in this absurd, inadequate version of being alive;
with a feeling of that maternal condescension,
so strange, yet so friendly,
of Nature that is something great and grand.

Rose of the Shadow

Who saw me or saw me not, the shadow saw me.
It came just then, a man-warm shadow, creeping
through my life, the door half open,
an ash-grey essence, unperfumed,
a wave where two eyes, made one, shone forth in
immensity.

Shadows: they see all round them, but never
acknowledge
our glances. They alarm us; but then, like oil,
remain invulnerably tranquil.

With their spirals winding in and out, and exact
foreshortening,
predicting every impossible act of espionage,
of insinuation and intervention.

Apprehensive yet fearless,
biting yet lipless,
they leave no obligation.

At times, they leave a rose behind them,
an ash-grey essence unperfumed,
sensual pledge of a faith left nameless.

Sombre rose of the shadows, and formed from shadow,
set within reach of my hand with an elegant gesture,
with soundless melody, with shame-faced laughter,
by something that could not see –
here in my hand I hold it.

I Would That All My Verses

I would that all my verses
could be such as the sky is in the night-time:
truth of the moment – now – without history.

That, like the sky, they would yield at every instant
all things, with all their streaming stars, and
neither childhood, nor youth, nor age could rob them,
nor cast a spell on the immensity of their beauty.

A thrill, a bright flash, music,
before my eyes and upon me!
The thrill, the bright flash, the music, right between my
eyes,
– the whole sky in my heart – the naked book!

Many a Pilgrim

God in our consciousness, You fall on the world
like a full kiss from a whole face,
to appease all desires.
The light of noon
reflects Your absolute splendour;
and to the furthest corner
You Yourself penetrate,
with joy in life's sublime possession.

Your presence against me
is Your natural sequence; and You are
my mirror spread in a vast embrace
(the mirror being oneself plus one),
leaving Your image joined to my image,
my image with Your image,
in an ember of fused completeness.

This is the decisive act
of my imagination in motion,
that I pondered one day on the sea,
on the sea of my life and of my death,
the sea of my awaited answer;
and this is the contrived mirage
of the straightest path
to my foreordained desire.

Through this stupendous fate,
amidst the forest of my springtime,
flows the electric current
of my hunted beauty,

that which returned, returns and will return again;
the rising succession of my ecstasy of glory.
This is the glory, glory only equal to this one,
the glory of You in me, the glory of me in You.

God; this is the sum total in song of the blessed
that many a pilgrim seeks.

Antonio Machado

Translated by Charles Tomlinson and Henry Gifford
with an Introduction by Henry Gifford

Introduction

Antonio Machado deserves to be more widely known outside the Spanish-speaking world. There his reputation stands higher than in his own lifetime. 'Today,' writes Luis Cernuda, 'when any poet comes to express his admiration for an earlier poet, it is usual for him to mention Antonio Machado.' The interesting anthology by José María Castellet, *Veinte años de poesía española* (1939–59), is dedicated to the memory of Machado, and the introduction gives him a commanding place. Machado beyond question is a poet having the stature and resonance of W. B. Yeats or Alexander Blok – that is to say, an unmistakably national poet who felt keenly the stresses and the tragic potentialities of life in a backward, suffering, fanatical country, and affirmed through the experience a larger truth that transcends patriotism. Thus they become European poets; and, indeed, the history of Spain, Ireland, and Russia as they felt and recorded it has much to say about the whole European dilemma.

The attraction of Machado, then, to the foreign reader lies at the beginning in his poetic concern with Spain. The volume of 1912, amplified in 1917, *Los campos de Castilla*, from which many of the versions that follow have been drawn, presents a Spain, and especially one focal part of it, Castile, which is already half familiar to us from our long acquaintance with Don Quixote, and from more recent memories of the Civil War. Written across this land is the title of Unamuno's great book, *The Tragic Sense of Life*, and Miguel de Unamuno the Basque and Antonio Machado the Andalusian were the two finest interpreters of Castile. Spaniards today, now that the problem of *castellanismo* which meant so much to 'the generation of '98' has grown stale, show perhaps some impatience with this side of Machado's work, and emphasize the delicacy and rare insight of his earlier poetry, the *Soledades* and *Galerías* (1907). Not long since, Juan Ramón Jiménez wrote that Antonio Machado comprised three poets: the pupil of Rubén Darío, the pupil of Gustavo Adolfo Bécquer (in his view the essential Machado), and lastly the 'popular' Antonio Machado himself, who wrote of and increasingly for the people, and publicized his gift. Whether we share Jiménez's misgivings about this third aspect or not, Machado the portrayer of Spain may have lately obscured his other self, the poet of dreams, paradoxes, and intimations.

With Machado's Spain, however, we must begin. It was a Spain shocked by losing the last vestiges of its empire in 1898, and until the Civil War broke out in 1936 far removed from the main business of Europe. Machado, born in 1875, qualified as a member of the celebrated 'generation of '98' and most of its best-known representatives were among his friends. He died in March 1939, just across the border in France, after sharing in the terrible exodus from Catalonia. Spain did not treat him at any time with special favour, though he had renown as a poet, and was early recognized by the admired Darío. Most of his life he spent as a teacher of French in country schools, and what this meant can be seen from the 'Poem of a Day' written in Baeza soon after he had moved from Soria in Old Castile after his wife's death. A letter to Unamuno of the same time is outspoken about the darkness and destitution of the place known as 'the Andalusian Salamanca': it had its schools, and a seminary, and a College of Art, but there was only one bookshop, which sold picture postcards, books of devotion, and pornography; a bare thirty per cent of the population could read; there was much show of religion but little piety; the peasantry was brutalized and broken, with no alternative but to emigrate 'in conditions amounting to suicide'. This, 'the richest district of Jaén', supported a population of beggars and small gentry ruined at the roulette table. All the misery of provincial life is held in the 'Poem of a Day', and its inanity in 'The Ephemeral Past'. Only Chekhov's Russia could show a similar waste and frustration.

He recognized, however, 'a spiritual superiority in the poor lands on the upper Duero' – the Soria where Machado lived for five years, married and soon lost his wife, and discovered the 'landscape of his soul', *tierra de su alma.* Eight years of childhood in Seville gave him the memory of a garden, with fountains and lemon trees, but his boyhood spent in Madrid and the decisive years at Soria replaced that vision by the mountains and stony fields, the ilexes and the silent figures in the Castilian solitude. It was Castile that had formed Spain, and here Machado could find a moral dignity born of endurance among the mountains.

His imaginary poet and pedagogue, Juan de Mairena, says that in the countryside the poet 'senses rhythms that do not accord with the flow of his own blood, and that are in general more slow' – planetary rhythms. The countryside 'compels him to feel the distances'. And it subdues the mind by its solitude and indifference: as Yvor Winters has written:

> in an empty place
> I met the unmoved landscape face to face;

or as Mairena continues:

> Those wonderful pinewoods, and those mountains of stone, which know nothing of us, however much we know of them! This has its charm, though it is also solemn cause for distress.

Machado did not go to the landscape like the townsman Rousseau: he sought there 'the countryman's emotion, essentially Georgic, for land that is worked'. The ilexes

are the field
and hearth
the tutelary shade
of the good villagers
who wear
brown serge
and cut for brands
your branches with their naked hands.

Seeing the old elm above the Duero, he meditates on its likely uses, as shaft, yoke, or fuel in a wayside cottage. When the cold rain is falling outside, he remembers 'the sowers of the grain'

and those who live
by gathering
the olive,
those who hope
for the fortune of a meal
and have
all that they own
in the year's deceitful wheel . . .

There is little joy in this landscape, any more than in the Flintcomb-Ash where Tess grubbed swedes, chilled by the rain and buffeted by the wind. Machado like Hardy sees man as 'slighted and enduring': words that apply to the ilexes of Castile and by analogy to the Castilian peasant.

Perhaps only a sensibility bred in Andalusia could have responded so richly to Castile, and with the same detachment. Its daunting rigours and military temper are played against the extravagance and tenderness of the south. Machado accepts Castile as a vocabulary of suffering, a means of survival after Leonor's death, and a source of the gravest poetry. Through Castile he comes into communication with the austere measures of the fifteenth-century poet Jorge Manrique, who set him a standard for true feeling and right expression. The severities of Castile and the calm fortitude of Manrique in the face of death inspire Machado to write an essential Spanish poetry at once familiar and new.

Poetry, he maintained, should come from the heart:

> Water
>   of the good spring
> fugitive
>   always; always living;
>   poetry –
> that cordial thing.

It should run freely, without ambition of technical display. Machado abhorred the baroque: the classical 'overcomes and eliminates' difficulty, he said, whereas the baroque parades it. He aimed first at directness, using metaphor only where plain statement had no resources. 'Good poets are sparing in the use of metaphors; but their metaphors at times are real creations.' Such indeed are Machado's: the wheel of the year; the draw-well that plunges into the shadowy depths; the river borne seawards (Manrique's river that becomes Machado's); the hardy ilex; the ageing elm that renews its foliage in spring. These are all images of subjection to time; and Machado's poetry can be defined as *temporal*.

In 1910 he attended the lectures of Henri Bergson at the Collège de France. Mr Eliot also went to them, and, like Machado, did not come away empty-handed. Machado, indeed, had been aware of Bergson's main preoccupations before this, but in common with many poets and writers of the age (Proust being the most notable) he found that

Bergson spoke to his own needs. Machado wrote a poetry dominated by time, which, as Mr Richard L. Predmore has shown,[1] penetrates almost every passage in his work. This 'dialogue of the poet with his time' relies on the verb, and disencumbers itself of ornament, including any but the freest rhymes, mainly assonantal. In a little poem called 'From My Notebook' Machado declares:

La rima verbal y pobre,
y temporal, es la rica.
El adjetivo y el nombre,
remansos del agua limpia,
son accidentes del verbo
en la gramática lírica
del Hoy que será Mañana,
del Ayer que es Todavía.

'Assonance (*la rima pobre*) when of the verb and temporal is the rich rhyme. Adjective and noun – still pools of clear water – are accidents of the verb in the lyric grammar of today which becomes tomorrow, of yesterday which still lasts.'

How yesterday can still last the imaginary poet Mairena demonstrates in a remarkably fine judgement of the merits of a sonnet by Calderón and a stanza from Manrique, both treating of mutability. Calderón's piece is static and plays with concepts disguised as images. Manrique asks 'what has become of the ladies, their head-dresses, their clothes, their perfumes?'

¿ Qué se hicieron las damas,
sus tocados, sus vestidos,
sus olores?

And after lamenting the vanished fires of love, and the music, he asks what has happened to *aquel danzar*, the parti-

1. *Publications of the Modern Language Association of America*, lxiii (1948), pp. 696–771: 'El tiempo en la poesía de Antonio Machado'.

cular dancing that went on, and *aquellas ropas*, the particular fashion they wore. 'When the stanza is over,' Mairena observes,

> all of it stays vibrating in our memory like a unique melody . . . The emotion of time is altogether there in Manrique's stanza; there is nothing, or next to nothing, of it in Calderón's sonnet. The difference is deeper than appears at first sight. It alone explains why in Manrique the lyric still has a future, and in Calderón, our grand baroque, a past done away with and dead once for all.

Poetry then should deal with particulars – *those* dresses, or *that* elm on a bend of the Duero – as they are located in time, and suffer its passage. The lines 'To a Dry Elm' show as complicated an awareness of time, past, present, and to come, as Coleridge's *Frost at Midnight*. The tree is described in its essential being, with knowledge of the past – the rains of April and the sun of May – and prediction about its future. The weight of the poem falls on verbs in a variety of tenses, as so often with Machado; the adjectives and the nouns are 'accidents of the verb', 'standing pools' on the way to the inexorable sea. Machado preferred the adjective that qualifies (from intuition) to the adjective that defines (which he associates with baroque and the death of imagination). His adjectives reveal the thing in its singularity, even when they appear most commonplace: the bushes in a village square outline

sus negras sombras en la arena blanca,

and these black shadows on white sand, like 'the moon in the zenith', and the illuminated clock on the church tower, inscape a particular moment. So the yellowish moss-stain on the dry elm, and the grey web of the spiders in its hollow, convey through colour the actuality of an experience. Colours – the white daisies, grey hills, or violet light – suggest the essence of what is described: through them the temporal seems to escape from time. One colour he associates with the permanence of Castile is *pardo*: 'brown', 'dun', or 'dusky', and it is applied to the earth of Soria, to rocks and mules and to nightingales in the poplars, to the light of evening, to the ilexes, and to the serge worn by the peasants. Often it conveys the idea of endurance. Men and creatures, for Machado as for Hardy, blend into a working landscape. The land, its people, and its divinities are one. The soil of Castile, *adusta* (parched), corresponds with the temper of its people (*adustez*, austerity); and the presiding deity of the landscape is *el Dios adusto*. In the same way the ilexes of Castile are *humildes*, lowly and enduring; so too is the meadow *humilde*, and the springtime; finally Castile itself, *la gentil, humilde y brava*.

The poem 'Lines to a Master' prescribes an ideal for Machado himself: brevity and power of apothegm facilitated by the language; all 'fruit of sense' (as Pope observed

> Words are like leaves; and where they most abound,
> Much fruit of sense beneath is rarely found);

verse that is at once lyrical and meditative, *se canta y medita* (Ortega had the virtue of being a *meditador*); perfection of the rhyme (after the style of Bécquer, whose 'pure and transparent verse' Machado much valued): a poetry disciplined, vigorous, and exact. While pretending to care little for form, in practice he constructed his poems most carefully: the 'Lament for Don Guido' in its conversational ease hides an incomparable dexterity. He achieves resonance and point, clarity and tenderness. In his poetry we encounter a mind that has accepted loneliness and yet seeks all the while to communicate. 'My heart always sings in chorus': the I must also collaborate with the Thou, and 'my feeling is not, in short, exclusively mine, but rather OURS'. Poetry leads out of solitude, and he counts on the genius of the language and on the old poets to help him. Cernuda has discerned the rhythms of Jorge Manrique throughout the 'Poem of a Day'. Machado like all original poets knew where to find what was living in tradition. When reading him we have to do not only with a gifted individual but with the Spanish language in its characteristic strength.

These versions seldom retain the metres of the original, yet they seek to correspond with its essential movement. Translating from a language which like Spanish is within the degrees of affinity because of the Latin elements in our own speech resembles the dialogue with the 'familiar compound ghost' in *Little Gidding*. The words 'compel the recognition they precede', and we are ourselves yet other in hearing them. The Spanish sensibility is not our own; yet it becomes accessible through the common awareness of Rome and the Roman qualities in language. Machado is not to be divorced from his tradition (of Manrique, Cervantes, the *Romancero*, Lope de Vega, Bécquer) which we cannot fully enter. Yet by bringing his verse into the borderlands of English, where it can be domiciled and yet stay foreign, we let him participate in our own literature. Translation saves no man from the duty of reading verse in its original tongue if he means fully to understand it. But through the services of translation our own language and its poetry can extend their awareness. Antonio Machado is a welcome guest to English poetry; a distinguished presence, rich in abilities; and an example to be felt and cherished.

HENRY GIFFORD

Childhood Recollection

The schoolboys are at work.
Beyond the window panes
where day is raw and light is weak,
monotony of winter rain.

In the classroom. Pictured
on a placard there is Cain
in flight, and Abel, dead,
next to a scarlet stain.

Thin, ill-clad and dry as tinder,
the ageing master rumbles on
in a sonorous and hollow thunder;
the book lies open in his palm.

The chanting of the lesson, and
from a whole choir of children:
a thousand hundreds – a hundred thousand,
a thousand thousands make a million.

The schoolboys are at work.
Across the window panes
where day is raw and light is weak,
monotony of winter rain.

Twelve Was Chiming . . .

Twelve was chiming . . . Twelve
blows of the spade in earth . . .
My hour! I cried . . . The silence
replied to me with: Do not fear.
You will never see
the last drop
poised in the water-clock.

On the familiar shore
still you shall go on sleeping many an hour,
and you will wake
to find your boat
tied on a clear morning
to another side.

Embers of a Violet Dusk . . .

Embers of a violet dusk
smoke on through the black of cypresses.
Enclosed by the shadowed arbour
stands the fountain with its nude
and winged stone Love
that dreams in silence. In the marble
basin the dead water does not move.

The Draw-Wheel

At its dusty and sad
ending, the day.

Water in time
to the slow draw-wheel's
buckets was chanting
its plebeian rhyme.

The mule was dreaming
the pitiful creature!
to the tune of shadow
that sounds in the water.

At its dusty and sad
ending, the day.

What poet incomparable
I cannot say, gave
like a god to the bitterness
of the wheel that is endless

the consonant sweetness
of the sounding of water,
and bound up its eyes
the pitiful creature! . . .

But that it was
a poet incomparable
god-like I know,
a heart well-seasoned
of wisdom and shadow.

Gloss

On a Passage from Jorge Manrique

We the rivers who supply
with transitory lives the sea
of death . . . what lines they are!

    Among my poets
Manrique has an altar.

Life's sweet fruition:
the evil certainty of passing
seaward with blind expedition.

First the terror death will bring
then the pleasure of arriving.

What pleasure! Yes . . .
yet in the horror
of recurrence? – what weariness!

O Luminous Late Day! . . .

O luminous late day!
The air's enchanted.
The white stork flying by
is half asleep
and the swallows
cross one another – wings
sharp-stretched
to the gold air –
and away
through the benign
distances of evening,
flying, dreaming.

And there is one
returns like the arrow – wings
sharp-stretched
to the sombre air –
bound for the roof
and its black corner there.

The white stork,
like a pot-hook,
tranquil and ungainly
so absurd!
looms on the belfry.

Guitar of the Roadside Inn

Today
You will dance and say
Aragon, Valencia!
tomorrow brings
an Andalusian hand
to explore your dusty strings
and Andalusia becomes your land.

Guitar of the roadside hostelry
a poet you never were, nor shall be:
you are a soul in stillness, speaking
its solitude to souls in flight:
entranced, the listening traveller
will catch an always native air.

Winter Sun

It's noon. A wintry park.
White paths. Symmetrical
little soil-heaps
and branches skeletal.

Orange shrubs in pots
under the conservatory,
and in its green-painted
barrel, the palm-tree.

Only his old cape hears
an old wizened man say:
'The sun! the beauty
of it.' The children play.

The water of the fountain
dreams, glides, runs
licking as though dumb
the weedy stone.

Portrait

Recollections of a patio in Seville,
a lucid, lemon-ripening garden – my infancy.
The years of my youth? Twenty on soil of Castile;
a plotlessness I shall not recall, my history.

Neither a seducer like Mañara,[1] nor a Bradomín,[2]
– you know already the incompetence of my dress –
but I took the arrow that Cupid had assigned,
and in the women I loved, I loved their hospitableness.

My verse comes up from an untroubled spring,
despite, in my veins, the drops of Jacobin blood;
and, more than the man who lived by mere doctrine,
I, in the good sense of the word, am good.

I adore beauty and in modern aesthetics
merely cut ancient roses from Ronsard's garden:
I dislike the glare of contemporary cosmetics,
and the nest of new singing birds has too gay a burden.

I disdain those ballads for the tenor, sonorous, hollow,
and the choir of the crickets singing at the moon,
I stop to distinguish the voices from the echo
and I listen among the voices to one alone.

1. Mañara: Miguel de Mañara Vicentelo de Leca (1629–79). After a dissolute youth, given over to all forms of luxury and excess, was miraculously converted. He appears to be the model for Angel Guerra in Galdós's novel of that name.

2. Bradomín: The Marqués de Bradomín, whose fictitious memoirs form the four *Sonatas* (1902–5) of Ramón del Valle-Inclán.

Classic or romantic? I cannot say. Let
me leave my verse as the captain leaves his sword:
known for the virile hand that flourishes it,
not prized for the learned craft of the smith who forged.

I talk with the man who is always there beside me
– he who speaks alone hopes one day to speak with
  God –;
the secret of Love for men: in my soliloquy,
discoursing with this good friend taught me this good.

And in the end I owe you nothing: you all remain
in my debt for what I've written. I work, I pay
with my own money for the clothes, the house I live in,
both the bread that nourishes and the bed in which I lie.

Once the day of the last voyage arrives, and there
the ship, that will not return to it, neighbours the quay,
you will find me aboard already, scanty of gear,
next to naked, like one of the kindred of the sea.

The Ilexes

Woods
of Castilian ilexes
on slope
and eminence
hillsides
and sudden fastnesses
woods, that
dense with a brown and brambled dark
are where
in the ilex tree
strength and humility agree.
As the axe
goes through
fills you with empty space
will no one
speak
ilex trees
to celebrate your qualities?
The oak is war
the oak
spells valour
mettle, rage immovable
that writhes
and ramifies –
a tree of caste
that, thewed and ruggeder
is more the master.

The tallness
of the oak
appears
to knot
compress
its hardiness,
an athlete who
sinks his rooted weight into
the soil below.
Pine is sea and sky
and mountain:
planet!
Palm:
the desert,
distance and the sun
the thirst, the cool
spring we dream of in
the rigid plain.
Who was it read
in the legendary beech
historic dread? –
battle
crime,
and who
has seen a beechwood in
a forest full of pine
and does not watch disquieted?
The poplars
are the riverbank
the lyres
of spring, beside
the slow or swift-
ly shifting flow

that spreads
        across the backwater
                or goes
contracted
        through tumultuous narrows.
                They imitate
in their eternal shivering
        the living waves
                of silver
at the river's spate.
        Elms
                in their parkland copses are
the good groves
        where
                Hope, bright-haired
must soon inherit
        the white
                of Contemplation.
The tree
        that bears it
                bears
the apple's scent;
        the aroma of its leaves
                cleaves
to the eucalyptus tree,
        to the orange
                fragrance of the flower;
and the garden's
        elegance is
                the dark unbending cypress's.
And you
        of the rustic stance? –
                the ashen trunk that has

neither grace nor arrogance
and branches
that are colourless;
'verdurous' would not
describe your leaves
(swart ilexes)
nor catch your vigour
without strain and your
humility that's firmness.
Nothing
shines
in the round
spread summit –
neither
your foliage
that's green-obscure
nor the yellow green
that marks your flower.
There's
nothing
handsome or superb
or warlike
in your bearing,
and in your mood
no petulance:
erect, awry
with that humility
that yields
only to the law of life,
you grow
and live
the best
that you know how.

The land itself
was turned into
a tree in you
brown ilex, burned
by the sun
and frost, by all
August and January
can do,
and you have stayed
constant
beneath the snowflakes and the threads
of rain,
made
(as it were) a pact
with the lands around
you, to remain
impassive
sound, serene
and sturdy –
ever-green:
and you have kept it
whether in Aragon
and its marches, or
where your darkness
perches on
Pamplona's military peaks;
and in
Extremadura,
in Castile
our Spain's
creator,
on level
ridge and mountain –

the plateau
encircled by
a youthful Duero
and along
the snaking Tagus through
Toledan land
and where
in Santandér
your way draws seaward.
A frank
frown of Castile
your dissonance was heard
in Moorish Córdoba,
and you are there
wooding Madrid,
stately and sombre
in the chill
of Guadarrama,
Castile's disdain
that must correct
the vanity, display
and fever
that infect the court:
I know
how the most distinguished
brushes have painted you
complete with greyhounds
and with chargers, how
Augustan poets
sang
and royal huntsmen made
you deaf with muskets: you
however, are the field

and hearth
    the tutelary shade
        of the good villagers
who wear
    brown serge
        and cut for brands
your branches with their naked hands.

Summer Night

Beautiful
the summer night:
fronting the rectangular
deserted, ample
village square,
tall houses
stand,
their balconies
unshuttered that command
a prospect of stone benches
of acacia and spindle-trees
that trace
symmetrically black
their shadows
on the white of sand.
Moon
in the zenith,
in the tower
the clock's
illumined sphere.
And I
in this old village
pass alone,
am phantomed by
its sharpness
its solidity.

To a Dry Elm

Sparsely
with a few green leaves
the old elm
breaks:
lightning, rot
could not gainsay
what rains of April
sun of May
at last bring out.
A century
it's held the height
above the Duero.
Moss-stain spreads
a yellow on the white
bark of its dusty trunk
the worm invades.
Unlike the poplars
singing guardians
of road and river
it will never be
to the tawny nightingales
their nesting tree.
In file
the military ants
go climbing over it:
within
the grey webs thicken as
the spiders spin.
Before the woodman fells
and you

are turned into
    a beam to stay a bell
        a shaft, a yoke,
before
    tomorrow when
        you'll smoke and redden
on a wretched, wayside
    hovel hearth,
        before
the whirlwind tear your roots
    or breath
        of white sierras
rend you or river
    send
        through gulch and valley to the sea
let me record
    this growing beauty branches stored:
        for how the heart
must read
    in what it sees
        its expectations'
life and light
    and echoing
        await
a second miracle of Spring!

Poem of a Day

Rural Meditations

Behold me
here – the nightingales'
apprentice, master
of *la gaya scienza*
formerly:
I teach
the living tongues
to a damp and bleak
sombre and straggling
village that belongs
half to La Mancha, half
to Andalusia.
Winter:
the fireside:
in the street
a fine rain falls
alternately as mist or sleet.
I
a husbandman in fancy
dream of fields.
O Lord,
how well thou dost
and how
it rains!
on vineyards and on olive-groves
fields of barley and of beans:
a still
a small and steady train.

How the sowers of the grain
will bless
like me
Your bounteousness,
and those who live
by gathering
the olive,
those who hope
for the fortune of a meal
and have
all that they own
in the year's deceitful wheel –
this
and every year that's gone.
Rain,
rain on!
and alternate
as mist or sleet
and then again
reverting to a tenuous rain
rain, Lord, rain!
My chamber keeps
a wintry light:
the afternoon
through rain and glass
sifts its grey illumination –
a medium where thoughts may pass.
The clock
neglected in its corner
looms distinct:
its tick
forgotten in its repetitions
now beats on
within my consciousness
and boring, bored

a uniform metallic heart
speaks its one and only part:
tick
tock:
in villages like these
does one catch
the pulse of time?
Truceless
before the clock
one, rather, fights
against monotony
that, in these villages
alights
to measure
the passage of their vacancies.
But, clock, is yours
this time of mine –
are mine your hours?
(Tick, tick)
There was a day
(tick, tick) that passed
and that which I
most loved
death made away.
A knell from far
fades
into the rain's
minute, untroubled chime
that rings against the window panes.
A husbandman in fancy
I
return to fields.
Lord,

how they'll bless
your bounteousness –
those
who sow the bread.
Lord,
is not the rain you bring
law in the ox-ploughed field
and in
the palace of the King?
Bounteous water,
leave
behind you, life –
you that go
drop by drop, and
spring by spring
and river upon river flow,
that, like this time
of weariness supply
the sea
with transitory life,
with all that seeks nativity
to germinate
to spring
and be.
Be
merciful
for you become
tomorrow's
early ear of grain, and
you restore
tint in the field
and in the flesh
and more:

reason
    madness
        bitterness
the grief that wishes for
    and yet remains unsatisfied
        with all belief.
Dark
    is coming down;
        the wire
reddens within the bulb
    gathering to a glow
        with scarce more show
than wax on a lucifer.
    God only knows
        where (under these tomes, reviews
and scribblings) –
    ah, here they are:
        my spectacles.
New books.
    One
        I open
by Unamuno.
    Oh, the chosen
        cherished spirit
of the Spain that shall inherit
    our coming life
        our resurrection!
This
    teacher of a country school,
        unheard of,
he knows no defection,
    Rector of Salamanca!
        Yours –

the philosophy you call
dilettante and inconstant
balanced
upon its slender rope –
nourishes, great
Don Miguel
his buried hope.
Water
of the good spring,
fugitive
always; always living;
poetry –
that cordial thing.
Architectonic?
(Do you look
for architecture
in the wind,
in the soul's structure?)
Rower,
sailor
across that sea
which has no shore.
Henri Bergson:
Les données
immédiates
de la conscience.
Is this
another Gallic artifice?
This Bergson
is a sell – agreed,
Maestro Don Miguel?
He's no Immanuel Kant –
it's the immortal somersault

his writings want;
this devilishly clever Jew
locates
free will
within his mind's own gates.
Ah, well –
every wise man has his problem,
every idiot his theme.
And yet
it still would seem
to matter whether
we, in a short and evil life
shall live
as either slaves or free.
But if
(as the poet shows)
it's seaward all our living flows –
all will come
to the same thing.
Oh, these villages!
reflections
readings
annotations
soon will end
in what they are:
the yawns
of Solomon.
Is it all
solitude of solitudes
vanity of vanities
as saith Ecclesiastes?
My waterproof,
umbrella

and sombrero:
the rain is moderating –
shall we go?
Night:
the talk is on
in the rear room
at the apothecary's
where they define
what makes the liberals such swine
and Don José
scents consolation
in the return (predicted)
of the conservative administration,
all spicing it
from the inexhaustible resources
of a people's wit:
'The past
and future
are the same.
Others
like us, will blame
the government.
All changes,
comes
and goes.' And then,
for arbitration:
'No evil lasts a century
to plague a nation.'
'And the beans
have come on splendidly –'
'These rains –'
'The barley –'
'And they'll flower

by March
unless the frost –'
'The labourers
will count the cost
in sweat –'
'Torrents –'
'Seas
would scarcely quench the thirst of olive trees.'
'In other days –'
'The rain would rain
at the Lord's will, then
as now.' 'Until
tomorrow, gentlemen.'
Tick
tock
tick-tock: one
day has gone
like any other
says the monotone of the clock.
My table bears
les données de la conscience
immédiates.
It's adequate
this I
that's fundamental
and at times
creative and original, that
mingling in mortality
its freedom and contingency,
can feel
can see, and yet
must overleap the confines
of its narrow keep.

Baeza, 1913

November 1913

Another year
has gone,
the sower casts
the seed in furrowed earth.
Oxen
plough
in two
slow pairs
whilst ashen clouds
pass over
shadowing
the plain,
the seed-fields
where there's nothing growing,
the grey
of olive-groves.
The river
deep in the valley
carries by
its troubled waters.
Snow
on Cazorla
and a storm
round Mágina,
Aznaitín has
his cloud-cap on:
mountains
bright towards Granada
mountains
made of stone
of light.

Lament of the Virtues and Verses on Account of the Death of Don Guido

It was pneumonia
finally carried away
Don Guido, and so the bells
(*din-dan*) toll for him the whole day.

Died Don Guido
gentleman; when younger
great at gallantry and roistering,
a minor talent in the bullring –
older, his prayers grew longer.

This Sevillan gentleman
kept (so they say)
a seraglio, was apt
at managing a horse
and a master
at cooling manzanilla.

When his riches dwindled
it was his obsession
to think that he ought to think
of settling in quiet possession.
And he settled
in a very Spanish way
which was – to marry
a maiden of large fortune
and to repaint his blazons,
to refer to the traditions of
'this house of ours',

setting a measure
to scandals and amours
and damping down the expenditure on pleasure.

He became, great pagan
that he was,
brother in a fraternity;
on Holy Thursday could be seen
disguised
(the immense candle in his hand)
in the long robe of a Nazarene.

Today
you may hear the bell
say that the good Don Guido
with solemn face
tomorrow must go
the slow road to the burial place.
For ever and for always
gone, good Don Guido . . .
'What have you left?' some will say –
I ask, 'What have you taken
to the world in which you are today?'

Your love for braid
and for silks and gold
and the blood of bulls and the fume that rolled
from off the altars.

To good Don Guido and his equipage
bon voyage!

The here
and the there,
cavalier,

show in your withered face,
confess the infinite:
the nothingness.

Oh the thin cheeks
yellow
and the eyelids, wax,
and the delicate skull
on the bed's pillow!

Oh end of an aristocracy!
The beard on breast
lies limp and hoary,
in the rough serge
of a monk he's dressed;
crossed, the hands that cannot stir
and the Andalusian gentleman
on his best behaviour.

The Ephemeral Past

Habitué of a small-town club, this man
who saw Carancha poised one day
to take the bull,
has a withered skin, hair going grey,
eyes dim with disenchantment, and beneath
the grey moustache, lips bent
in nausea and a look
that's sad – yet sadness it is not
but something more, and less: the void
of the world in the hollow of his head. He still
sports a jacket coloured currant-red
in a three pile velvet, breeches
booted at their extremities and a caramel
Córdoba hat, turned and furbished well.
Three times he inherited, then lost the lot
three times at cards and twice
was widowed. An illegal round of chance
alone will make him brighten
sprawled at the green baize table;
once more the blood begins to flow
as he recollects a gambler's luck
or the afternoon of some torero,
drinks in an episode from the life
of a daring bandit of the road
or the bloody prowess of a knife.
He satirizes with a yawn the government's
reactionary politics and then
predicts the liberals will come to power
again, just as the stork returns to the bell-tower.

Something of a farmer still, he eyes
the heavens, fears them and at times will sigh
thinking of his olives and, disconsolate,
watches for weather-signs when rain is late.
For the rest, boredom. Taciturn, hypochondriac,
shut in the Arcadia of the present,
and to his brow
only the movement of the smoke gives now
its look of thought. This man is neither
of yesterday nor tomorrow
but of never. Hispanic stock, he's not
the fruit that grew to ripen or to rot,
but shadow-fruit
from a Spain that did not come to be,
that passed away, yet, dead,
persists to haunt us with a greying head.

Grey Olives

Grey olives
bleached track.
The sun has drained back
the colour of the plain;

and the evil days'
essence of dust
into her memory
dries downwards through me.

To José María Palacio

Palacio,
good friend,
is spring
already clothing
the branches of the poplar trees
on road and river?
In the plain
of the upper Duero
spring
comes so slowly
but when she comes
she is all sweetness! . . .
The old elms,
have they
any new leaves?
As yet
the acacias will be bare,
and under snow
the mountains of the sierras.
Oh, there
in the sky of Aragon
the so beautiful
white and rose
mass of Moncayo!
Are the thorns
in flower among grey rocks
and are
white daisies there
in the delicate grass?
By now

storks will have been
      arriving on those belfries.
            There will be
greens of the coming wheat,
      a going
            of brown mules
into fields prepared for sowing
      and of the peasants
            who plant late crops
with the rains of April.
      Already
            bees
will broach
      the thyme and rosemary.
            Are plum trees
into blossom, do
      violets
            remain there too?
Stealthy,
      with lures for the partridge
            under a length of cloak,
huntsmen will not be absent.
      Palacio,
            good friend,
do the riverbanks
      hold nightingales already?
            On a blue
afternoon, the first
      roses and first lilies
            in the gardens,
go
      climb Espino:
            airy Espino where *her* country is.

To the Young Thinker José Ortega y Gasset

The laurel and the ivy wreath!
to you, the gods' elect
must fall
(Sophia's architect)
this coronal.
Chisel, hammer, stone
and masons serve you!
May cold Guadarrama's peaks
to you alone
who, sombre, think a new Escurial
proffer their deepest blue of all.
And may the austere Philip loom
to bless beside his royal grave
tomorrow's architecture
and the progeny that Luther gave.

Solitary Olive Tree

Beyond the grove
beside the spring
solitary olive tree
whose shadows bring
(olive of hospitality)
shelter to the thoughtful man
to the translucent water;
by the white edge of the way
may she bless
(olive of antiquity)
your greenness with her eyes' sea-grey
Athena, goddess!

from *Galerías*

Blue mountains, river, the erect
and coppery wands
of poplars in their delicacy,
and on the hill, the almonds white –
oh, snow in flower, butterfly in tree!
A bean-scent on its breath,
the wind goes by
runs in the plain whose solitude is gay.

Waters

(from *Proverbs and Canticles*)

I

Sun in the Ram. My window
stands open to cold air.
Evening wakens the river –
hark! the rumour of the water there.

II

Gregarious sound begins to wane
within the ancient hamlet, storks
crowning its ample turrets. In the plain
the water speaks from solitude and rocks.

III

As before, my thought
is water's captive;
but of water in the live
rock that is my heart.

IV

Can you tell the water's sound?
Whether of summit or of valley,
plaza, garden, orchard ground?

Further Proverbs and Canticles

I

The mode of dialogue, my friends,
is first to question:
then . . . attend.

II

I have seen in my solitude
very clear things
that are not true.

III

The poet does not pursue
the fundamental I
but the essential you.

IV

Let us give time to time:
that the vessel overflow
first you must let the water brim.

V

In writing verses, seek
to give them a double light: one
to read square by, one oblique.

VI

Let it not signify
whether they pass from hand to hand:
from gold men make a currency.

VII

This, to ponder:
a heart that's solitary
is a heart no longer.

Guadalquivír

Oh, Guadalquivír!
in Cazorla I saw you a spring;
today, dying in Sanlúcar.

A gushing of clear water
under a green pine
you were: how keen your chime!

Like myself, close to the sea,
river of brackish mud, do you
dream of your source's clarity?

Lines to a Master

I

Professor, not of energy
Francisco de Icaza
but of melancholy.

II

An ancient stem
transmits his brevity of word
his depth of apophthegm.

III

He's like the olive grove:
small shade beneath,
all fruit above.

IV

In his clear verse, you'll hear
both thought and song
flow without fret or fear.

V

And in perfect rhyme
– thus the river's twofold poplar
at the water's brim

VI

His cantos bear
water of standing pools,
stillness unyielding there.

And yet it does:
certain and seawards,
without haste it goes.

VII

His songs possess
(present gist of old affections)
aromas and aloe's bitterness.

And from the favour
of the Indian sun
fruit in ripeness and rich savour.

VIII

Francisco de Icaza, you
who span two Spains –
the Old and New,

a hundred réal piece must hold
beside your lyre
your viceroy's profile cut in gold.

A Penguin Classic

THE JEWISH POETS OF SPAIN

Translated by David Goldstein

Ha-Levi's yearning for the land of Israel, Gabirol's communion with his own soul, Moses ibn Ezra's grief in his exile, and the extraordinary martial character of Samuel ha-Nagid, Vizier to the Moorish King of Granada: each of these poets is represented in this anthology of Hebrew verse in Spain from the tenth to the thirteenth centuries. Their subjects range from a wine-feast in a beautiful hanging garden to the arcane treasures of immortality; and they bring together two strands of the civilization of the Jews, one the unbridled sensuality of the Song of Songs, the other the unshakeable faith of the Prophets.

A Penguin Classic

TWO SPANISH PICARESQUE NOVELS

Lazarillo de Tormes The Swindler

Translated by Michael Alpert

The social conditions of Spain in the sixteenth and seventeenth centuries bred the picaresque novel, which replaces the romantic hero with a rascally figure living by his wits. *Lazarillo de Tormes* (1554), the first and best of these essays in realism, describes the ingenious ruses employed by a boy from Salamanca to outwit his various masters. *The Swindler* (1626), by Francisco de Quevedo, represents the genre at its most sophisticated and witty in its account of the scatological adventure of a young servant who eventually sets up as a fake *hidalgo* in Madrid and earns his living by card-sharping.

Penguin Modern European Poets

This series now includes selected work by the following poets, in verse translations by, among others, W. H. Auden, Lawrence Ferlinghetti, Michael Hamburger, Ted Hughes, J. B. Leishman, Christopher Middleton and David Wevill:

Amichai
Apollinaire
Bobrowski/Bienek
Celan
Ekeiof
Enzensberger
Four Greek Poets:
Cavafy/Elytis/Gatsos/Seferis
Grass
Guillevic
Haavikko/Tranströmer
Holan
Holub
Kovner/Sachs
Montale
Pavese
Pessoa
Popa
Quasimodo
Rilke
Three Czech Poets:
Nezval/Bartušěk/Hanzlík
Ungaretti
Weöres/Juhász
Yevtushenko

Penguin Modern Poets

1* Lawrence Durrell Elizabeth Jennings R. S. Thomas
2* Kingsley Amis Dom Moraes Peter Porter
3* George Barker Martin Bell Charles Causley
4* David Holbrook Christopher Middleton David Wevill
5† Gregory Corso Lawrence Ferlinghetti Allen Ginsberg
6 George MacBeth Edward Lucie-Smith Jack Clemo
7* Richard Murphy Jon Silkin Nathaniel Tarn
8* Edwin Brock Geoffrey Hill Stevie Smith
9† Denise Levertov Kenneth Rexroth William Carlos Williams
10 Adrian Henri Roger McGough Brian Patten
11 D. M. Black Peter Redgrove D. M. Thomas
12* Alan Jackson Jeff Nuttall William Wantling
13 Charles Bukowski Philip Lamantia Harold Norse
14 Alan Brownjohn Michael Hamburger Charles Tomlinson
15 Alan Bold Edward Brathwaite Edwin Morgan
16 Jack Beeching Harry Guest Matthew Mead
17 W. S. Graham Kathleen Raine David Gascoyne
18 A. Alvarez Roy Fuller Anthony Thwaite
19 John Ashbery Lee Harwood Tom Raworth
20 John Heath-Stubbs F. T. Prince Stephen Spender
21* George Mackay Brown Norman MacCaig Iain Crichton Smith
22* John Fuller Peter Levi Adrian Mitchell
23 Geoffrey Grigson Edwin Muir Adrian Stokes

* *Not for sale in the U.S.A.*
† *Not for sale in the U.S.A. or Canada*